Joy Through the Pain

Gloria L. Mills Battle

Published by KB Designs & Publishing

ISBN: 978-1-312-61673-8

Cataloging –in-Publication Data is on file with the Library of Congress

SPECIAL SALES

Books are available at special discounts for bulk purchases for sales promotions or premiums. For more information, visit, http://www.lulu.com to contact the author for book signings.

Contents

Dedication:

Weeping may go on all night, but Joy comes in the morning. Psalm 30:5

I would like to dedicate this book to my loving Mother, Alma Parks Mills for her courage, strength, and her unconditional love. To my beautiful daughter, Kisha M. Battle Morris, and to my cousin, Dorothy A. Mills Gage; the two of you have inspired me to write and publish this book.

Foreword:

As I scan through the pictures of my Granny Mills, I can only give all praises to God for this wonderful, God-fearing woman who has always shown true strength, grace, humility, respect and reverence in all things. Growing up, I would always look forward to visiting my grandmothers but I would especially enjoy visiting Grandmother Mills. I would help her iron clothes for loose change, cook her toast and make her hot tea before going to work for the Runions, help make the beds, sweep the floors, vacuum and hang clothes out to dry. At the time, I didn't know what she was instilling in me, but now I know, all too well now that I have my own family, that to always put "love" in all that you do.

There were very few times that I can recall that Granny would raise her voice and her gentleness permeated through her solid frame. I loved her gentle demeanor and I wanted to be just like her. I would call her as much as I could after growing up just to talk to her and to see how she was doing. She was always "doing alright" and I looked forward to hearing her voice on my birthdays also. Each summer, I learned something new from her and I would ask many questions that she would either answer in some old time religion fashion or simply say that God has got the whole world in His hands. I loved singing this song with Granny Mills.

Throughout my teenage years, Granny Mills would always encourage me to "look to the hills from whence cometh my help" and I vowed to do just that. She would always tell me that I was special and that I would be something in the world. And I'd say, "I'm going to be a star!" This was our relationship. Granny Mills would often ask me to sing "Amazing Grace" to her friends while visiting the sick and shut in from the church or to my great-grandmother Mama Parks. My great Uncle Johnny would always tease me that I was going to be a famous singer and I would always tell him that he was right.

These were the times that I relish the most; my summertime Granny that would discipline me softly and sternly but would keep God close by to help me to understand the lesson being taught. I didn't get into too much trouble because I respected my Grandmother just that much. I wanted to protect her from all harm, hurt and danger; and that I did every summer. I felt like I was her guardian angel at times when she needed the most. There were several times when I would get scolded, and she would take the brunt of the scolding for me insisting that I was just a child and needed mean any harm in my sassiness. I love my Grandmother for this just because she stood up for me when I couldn't. I know that this was often difficult especially because Granny grew up in a different age and time and it took me the longest to truly understand reverence and respect in the family hierarchy.

I will never forget the summer YMCA camps, trips to Lake Junaluska, Sunday School at Bethel United Methodist Church in Greer, South Carolina, the shopping trips to Belk, Dollar General and the walks to Lil' Cricket before and after church to get .01 cent bubble gum. We had so much fun with our cousins during these summers to last a lifetime. I learned how to enjoy life, have fun and also to love the Lord with all my heart. I thank my Granny Mills for that. She has helped to shape me into the woman that I am today. I still feel and see the gentle grace and mercy that God has laid upon her in all her pictures from the beginning until now. As we age, we all lose a little of ourselves whether it's Dementia, Alzheimer's or any illness.

The bible tells us in Ecclesiastes 3,

A Time for Everything

3 There is a time for everything,
and a season for every activity under the heavens:

2   a time to be born and a time to die,
a time to plant and a time to uproot,
3   a time to kill and a time to heal,
a time to tear down and a time to build,
4   a time to weep and a time to laugh,
a time to mourn and a time to dance,
5   a time to scatter stones and a time to gather them,
a time to embrace and a time to refrain from embracing,
6   a time to search and a time to give up,
a time to keep and a time to throw away,
7   a time to tear and a time to mend,
a time to be silent and a time to speak,
8   a time to love and a time to hate,
a time for war and a time for peace.

9 What do workers gain from their toil? 10 I have seen the burden God has laid on the human race. 11 He has made everything

beautiful in its time. He has also set eternity in the human heart; yet no one can fathom what God has done from beginning to end. [12] I know that there is nothing better for people than to be happy and to do good while they live. [13] That each of them may eat and drink, and find satisfaction in all their toil—this is the gift of God. [14] I know that everything God does will endure forever; nothing can be added to it and nothing taken from it. God does it so that people will fear him.

[15] Whatever is has already been,
and what will be has been before;
and God will call the past to account.

[16] And I saw something else under the sun:

In the place of judgment—wickedness was there,
in the place of justice—wickedness was there.

[17] I said to myself,

"God will bring into judgment
both the righteous and the wicked,
for there will be a time for every activity,
a time to judge every deed."

18 I also said to myself, "As for humans, God tests them so that they may see that they are like the animals. **19** Surely the fate of human beings is like that of the animals; the same fate awaits them both: As one dies, so dies the other. All have the same breath; humans have no advantage over animals. Everything is meaningless. **20** All go to the same place; all come from dust, and to dust all return. **21** Who knows if the human spirit rises upward and if the spirit of the animal goes down into the earth?"

22 So I saw that there is nothing better for a person than to enjoy their work, because that is their lot. For who can bring them to see what will happen after them?

New International Version (NIV)

God has blessed us with my Grandmother Mills for such a time as this. I love being a part of her season and I know that God has purposed her in my life to build me up in character, grace, strength, goodwill and to know and love the Lord, our God, with all my heart. I know that my Mother, my Grandfather Mills, her children and her siblings feel the same sentiments as I do. May this memoir serve as a reminder to all of us of Alma Parks Mills legacy and life of love forever. She is such a "Gift of God".

Her Granddaughter,

Kisha Battle Morris

In the Beginning...

Georgia Girl Straight from
Lincolnton, Georgia

This story tells a true story about the life and memories I have shared with my Mother, Alma Parks Mills, and my best friend.   Mom has now reached the age of eighty-eighty years old. Lately I'm

having some difficulties dealing with my Mother having Dementia. This is a disease that attacks the brain.

For my peace of mind, I wanted to share some of my life experiences as a young girl and now as a woman;

about the wonderful relationship I shared with my Mom.

It was around June of 2007, when I noticed how my

Mother was changing. We have been so close all of these

years. My Mother is a kind and caring woman of God.

Mom has given so much of herself to everyone.

Mom has shown so much love to everyone. She

has given me so much wisdom on many things in my life. I

thank God for our long talks about life; some good and some not so good. This truly is a testimony on what God can do to restore a Christian relationship with a love one. It doesn't matter where you are in your relationship with your parents. It's never too late to start all over and rebuild that love.

Mom was raised by her parents Willie and Alberta Parks in Lincolnton, Georgia. Mom was born November 9, 1925. Mom is the oldest of her siblings. She graduated high school. After high school, Mom taught school at her home church, Mulberry C.M.E. Church School.

Mom left Georgia at an early age. She told me that one of her friends was raped. My grandparents were upset and decided to send Mom to live with someone else in South Carolina. They wanted a better life and education for her. Mom left Georgia to continue her education. She attended a two year college and received her degree in Rock Hill, South Carolina. Later on, she would begin teaching at Dunbar Elementary School in Greer. Mom taught there for a few years. As I recall, Mom told me that she was hired by the principal, Mr. Bankhead. Back in those days you didn't have to complete a four year college to teach.

Mom enrolled me in school at the age of five. The other kids would tease me that Mom was really hard on them. As far as I could see, Mom was the best in my eyes. Mom was from Lincolnton Georgia and proud it. She would always talk about her life and family in Georgia. Mom often spoke about her Father and Mother. She says now that her Mother and Father are gone on be with the Lord. It wouldn't be a week that would go by, when I didn't call home during my single days. Mom once shared with me that she changed for name from Mabel to Alma. Mom said she didn't like her name and decided to change it when she first came to South Carolina to live.

Mom has worked hard most of her life. She shared with me how she used to pick cotton in the fields from sun up to sun down. I recall once that Mom took me to pick cotton with her. I really didn't like this job. Instead of picking cotton, I played all day in the field. On any given day, Mom could pick over five-hundred pounds of cotton.

Alberta Jones Parks, Mama Parks

Mama Parks was Mom's mother. She loved her Mother. They had a very close relationship. I recall visiting my grandparents when they lived in Dodson in Greer then she and my Uncle Johnny moved to Greenville. Many times I would ride over to visit with my Mom, Mama Parks and Johnny when I came to town. I really enjoyed those visits with my Mama Parks.

Mom and Mama Parks talked on the phone almost every day. And there wasn't anything that she wouldn't do for her Mother. I recall on the day that my grandmother passed away, I was here in Maryland in my down stairs basement ironing some clothes. I felt somewhat strange

that day. When Mom called me to give me the news, I had already felt that I would get some sad news on this day. After the call I prepared to go home for her Homegoing service. Things would never be the same. I really don't know how Mom felt, but I do know for sure that a part of her died too; the day that my Mama Parks left us to be with the Lord. Mom really didn't talk much about how she felt.

Mom's Siblings

It's strange sometimes how things happen in our lives. Mom is the oldest of her siblings.   Mom had a special relationship with all of her siblings. As far as I know they all looked up to Mom. Listed below are her siblings who have passed on; Joe, S.T (Sweet), Alice, Christine (not shown), George (not shown), Eunice, Johnny, and two children who died at birth.

Mom now has only three siblings left, Aunt Rita (not shown), Bobbie, and Uncle Cornell (not shown). Mom was sad, and would often say, most of my family is gone. Aunt Bobbie still lives locally and Mom visits often. I never knew how it affected Mom when she lost her siblings. She never spoke about it. Sometimes I wonder if it was too much for her to bear.

Mom's Courtship & Marriage

Mom often spoke about her courtship to my Father, Garvin Mills. She was so funny telling this story. Mom was dating two young men at the time. She would go to church with my Dad in the morning, but in the afternoon she would attend church with another gentleman, whom I shall call, James. James was sweet on Mom.

I can't remember her saying how long she dated the other guy. I'm not sure if she was sweet on him, but she loved the attention that she was getting. Mom also talked about while she was dating Dad, she would have to do chores like plowing the field with the mule. Mom said that she would be so embarrassed that she would run off until Dad passed by.

That was the funniest story. She spoke about Dad asking her to wait on him until he returned from the war. Mom did wait on Dad. Today, they have marriage for sixty- eight years plus and the rest is history.   Thank God for everlasting love. Dad and Mom were married on October 20, 1946. They still reside at the same residence for all of these years.

Mr. and Mrs. Garvin & Alma Mills

Married October 20, 1946

Eastern Star Organization

I can't remember when Mom joined Eastern Star. She was proud to belong to this group of Christian women of God. Mom would put on her white uniform to attend her weekly meeting. She would be dressed from head to toe in white. During the holiday season, Eastern Star organization would have an annual event. Mom was excited to put on her beautiful after-five or evening gown for a grand time.

Oh how I wanted to join the Eastern Star and still do. I thought what a wonderful group that she belongs too. Mom served in the Eastern Star for more than thirty years. She is now inactive due to her illness. One day, Mom I shall follow in your footsteps.

Soul Food, Hot Meals and the Holidays

Mom was an awesome cook. Back in the day, we didn't eat much fast food. Mom prepared hot meals for us every day. I can remember Mom preparing fried sweet potato jacks for us before we left for school. Oh boy, that was a treat. When times were difficult we had to take our lunch to school in a paper bag. I really hated that but I never complained. But on Sunday, Mom would prepare the best meal of the week: fried chicken, macaroni & cheese, green beans, fresh greens, fried fresh corn, okra, hot biscuits, sweet potato pies and iced tea. It was all home-made fresh from the garden. We may not have had more than most families, but we had what our parents could provide for us. Mom would take the chicken and cut it into many pieces. You know until this day I don't know how she did it, but it was God who made all of that possible.

For Thanksgiving and Christmas, we had a turkey with all the trimmings. Those were the best times. For New Year's dinner, Mom would prepare chitterlings, collard greens, potato salad and black-eye peas. This was a family tradition.

Mom opening gifts during the Christmas holiday

Mom's Talents

Mom has many talents. She enjoyed cooking, sewing, croqueting hats, scarves, and blankets. Mom made several items for our families. It was Mrs. Elizabeth Scipio who taught Mom how to croquet. On one occasion, I came home for the weekend, Mom wanted to teach me the basic steps of croqueting. At first I didn't want to learn, but I thought why not.

I still know the basic steps to croqueting and still work at it sometimes. Mom did do some sewing. She would make aprons to wear when she worked at Victor Mill. When I would come to visit, Mom would ask me to make some aprons and she sold them to some of her co-workers. She is wearing a crocheted hat in this picture.

Ms. QVC- Fashion Queen

Let me tell you why, I call Mom, Ms. QVC. Mom was known to me as Ms. QVC of Greer. She finally got it. In the earlier years, Mom didn't focus on buying much for herself because all she wanted was to make sure that we had what we needed. Once the kids left home, it was only then that she started shopping for clothes. Mom enjoyed shopping

from the Shop-at-Home network. It was her time. She purchased some beautiful clothes. Oh boy, did I have fun in

Mom's closet.

Most of the time, Mom would find me something in her closet to bring back to Washington, D.C. I do cherish the times that we had together. Mom always had a giving spirit, but that was my Mom who gave so much of herself. I kept her supplied in fashion scarves that I had for her. Mom wanted to match everything. I guess that's where I got my fashion style from. She is now still known as the "Hat Lady". She has always worn a hat on her head. Mom loved croqueting her knit hats. She would also purchase church hats as well. I sure do get her style for wearing hats. Even with her Dementia, she has to have a hat on her head every day. Don't even try to take those hats away from her.

Mom's Best Friends

As I recall, Mom had a few close friends but there were two or more ladies that come to mind. She always spoke about Ms. Bessie Norris, Millie Super and Mrs. Jessie Logan. They didn't visit much, but called each other regular basis. They socialized at church and traveled to and from church meetings. I would come home to visit and Ms. Jessie would be on the phone. Mom's eyes would light up when Ms. Jessie called.

Two of these ladies have gone on to be with the Lord, but I know for sure that they had some great times together. When I first started doing by business in Mary Kay Cosmetics, I had a Mary Kay party. I invited some of the ladies that she attended church with along with some of our family members. Mom would often tell me that all of her closest friends are gone. I would tell Mom that God has left her here for a reason. Mom felt alone at times without her close friends.

Mom's Best friend Ms. Jessie Logan, during a photo shoot at a Mary kay show in Greer at the home of Betty Drummond.

Working as a Maid and Proud of it

I recall when Mom stopped teaching, she gained employment as a domestic worker. In other words, she worked as a maid. Sometimes Mom would take me along to help her clean. She taught me the proper way to make up a bed. One of the first families that Mom worked for was the Dodson's and later she would work for the Booster family.

Mom enjoyed what she did and always did her best. They treated her fair, as far as I know. Mom never complained about her employer. The next opportunity that came along was working at the Victor Textile Mill. Back then it was difficult for a black woman to work there, because they had to do the same job as the men who were employed there.

As Mom would mention, it was hard work for a woman. I recall Mom telling me that she was one of the first Afro-American women to work at Victor Mill. It was, as usual, that most of the Black employers worked on the midnight shift, from four to midnight. I really missed Mom working at night, but she had to do what she needed to do for her family. Mom said the pay was great. Mom worked hard at this job. She was saving money to help educate her children.

I remember Mom telling me that someone in the office wanted to know why she was taking so much money to go into to her Savings. Mom told her that the Savings was for her son's education. I don't remember how long Mom worked at Victor because I was no longer living at home. Many years would pass during Mom's employment, but the mill work was taking its toll on her health. Mom was diagnosed with a back condition and had to have back surgery.

I was away at the time when Mom had back surgery, but I came home after she got home from the hospital. Mama Parks had to come over and help take care of her once she was release from the hospital. This was a long recovery. I thank God that she made it through the surgery okay. That was the end of Victor Mill, because she wasn't able to do the work that she once did. Mom had to retire from the job.

Working for the Runion Family

It would be years later before Mom would go back to work. It was my cousin Dorothy, who worked for the Runions. Dorothy could no longer work for them, so she referred Mom for the job. Now Mom was doing domestic work again. The family was wealthy. They treated Mom alright. It was as if we had gained another family. When I spoke with Mom on the telephone that's all that she talked about was the Runions.

She loved working for the Runions. Mom helped take care of three children in the household, Travis, Charlie, and Mills. She also did housework as well. Mom would often travel with the family to their summer home. Mom shared with me this story about Charlie as a young child. Mom was taking care of Charlie, and asked him to come out from under the table, before he needed changing. Mom said she told Charlie, "If you don't come out from under that table, I'm going to spank you".

Mr. Runion said to Mom, "Ms. Alma are you going to spank my boy"? Mom replied, "Yes I am. If I'm to take care of him, he has to mine me". And that was that. Mom never had any other problems with Charlie again. Mom told me that Travis, Charlie, and Millie always gave her the utmost respect. She told me many stories about working with the Runions. Mom worked with the Reunions for twenty-five years plus. As Mom got older, they didn't allow her to do as much.

Mom had planned to work longer but due to an accident, she had to stop working and retire. On many days, Ms. Kathy would take her shopping. Mom loved that. On one occasion, I went by to pick Mom up from work and met them. Mom was invited to the youngest child, Millie's wedding. She couldn't wait to tell me about the wedding. Travis and his family came often to visit Mom after she left.

Mom and I talked often, she mentioned to me that Mr. Reunion said that if she out lived him that he would give her an allotment for each year that she had worked for them. Mr. Reunion passed away several years ago. The promise wasn't kept.

After Mom left the Runions, I stayed in touch with the family. Once Mom was diagnosed with Dementia, I called Charlie and the family to let them know. I told Charlie what Mom had told me about the allotment that Mr. Runion promised her.   Charlie told me that he really didn't know anything about the promised that Mr. Runion made. Charlie asked me if we wanted to put Mom in a nursing home and I replied no.

Mom had always told me that she never wanted to go into a nursing home. I told Charlie to do what the Lord would have him do. Charlie replied that he would call me back. I was home visiting Mom at the time. He did call me back with great news that they would give Mom an allotment for as long as she lives. Mom was so excited; all of her hard work had paid off. Charlie and his family still give Mom a gift certificate every year to purchase a turkey or a ham.

Memories of the Earlier Years

Growing up in Greer, SC

The highlight of our weekends would be when Mom would take us shopping on Saturday in Downtown Greer. Those were the best days. I also recall going to the bakery, to purchase cake cuttings for about ten cents a bag. At that time, that was a treat. I guess that's why I love sweets. We would go uptown to shop at Leader's department store.

As a young girl, sometimes I would feel so

embarrassed about how Mom was dressed. I wondered why Mom wouldn't fix herself up. I didn't realize at the time, but now I understand

why. Times were difficult, but Mom would take the extra money to make sure that we got what we needed. That truly is a Mom's love. Mom worked hard to educate the kids that wanted to continue their education with going off to college. I was only thinking about Mom, because it was difficult enough for her to send three of us off to college at one time. Once most of us were out of the house, Mom started buying things for herself.

During Some Chores for Cash

Mom worked during the day, so she assigned some chores for us to do.   During my high school years I had chores to do. One of my chores that I disliked was washing dishes. I felt like I was the only child that would have to wash dishes, I guess because I was the oldest girl.

One of the chores, I did do, was to iron up Dad's shirts for cash. I would count them out to earn money for myself. Mom would give me twenty-five cents per shirt. I wanted to earn money to go shopping. One of the other chores I did enjoy was washing clothes. We had an old fashioned washing machine with a roller on the top.

I was trying to wash clothes that day, when I accidently got my arm stuck in the washing machine rollers. I remember it like it was yesterday, Mom came running out to see if I had broken my arm. I didn't much want to wash clothes after that. I recall one time before that it was in the summer time Mom called me in to teach me how to cook. I was not interested in learning how to cook. I just complained the entire time, until Mom sent me out to play. Now that I look back, those cooking lesson were to prepare me for the real life. I wasn't looking that far ahead.

It's Church Time
BETHEL UNITED METHODIST CHURCH

Mom always carried us to Sunday school and church every Sunday. She always told us to get our clothes ready the night before. At that time we weren't allowed to iron on Sunday. Still strange enough, I still prepare my clothes for church the night before. I guess what Mom did teach me, back in the day, has stuck with me even now.

Mom is a strong Christian woman of God. When Mom joined the union of marriage with my father, Garvin, she became a member of Bethel United Methodist Church. She was very active at Bethel, where she taught Sunday school. Mom was a past President of the United Methodist Women. She has always been dedicated to her church. One year the church had a rally to raise money for the church. Mom and her group raised the most money and Mom was crowned Ms. Bethel. I was so proud of Mom. I thank God for her faith and love for God. She planted the seed for me to follow, and now, I have chosen to follow after God, to be a work in progress, and to be the best Christian that I can be.

A Mother's Advice
TEENAGE YEARS

Many times after I left home, I continued to call
Mom for advice. On one of my visits, I experienced a
problem with a young man that I was dating disagreed and
became angry with me. He decided to put his hand on me
and threaten me in my own home. The young man left
before my parents got home. I was upset. When Mom
returned home from work, I explained to her what
happened. On that night, Mom gave me some advice on
dating. She told me that if a man is treating you that way
and you are not married to them, you can imagine what he
will do to you when he gets you. Now that I think about it,
some of it was my fault as well. But Mom told me that he
still didn't have a reason to put his hands on me. Mom
told me that night to let this young man go. I listened to
Mom. And the rest is history. Mom never told me
anything that didn't help me during my life experiences.
During some of my life experiences Mom didn't always
agree with me. I thank God for her advice in guiding me in
the right direction. I always called home to talk to Mom.

Our relationship became even closer after I became engaged.

Picture of Lincoln High School Pageant

Trips Home to Greer, SC

Time would pass and I would go visit Mom. I
visited often. I started visiting on Mother's Day and
summers when I could. I used to visit for the Christmas
holiday
until I
began my
family. I
remember
speaking
with Mom
on the

phone non-stop. Mom loved her life. I noticed early on
that Mom would sit there on the sofa and read her
address book from front to back.

One thing I can say is that Mom sent all of her
family member's birthday cards and gifts. I would tell
Mom that the family is getting larger and maybe she
should stop giving everyone Christmas gifts. Mom told me
that she wanted to share what God had given her. So
Mom continued to share as much as she could.

Mom's Blessing, I'm Engaged

It was December 1969. I had to make a call to give
Mom the good news that I had gotten engaged. I couldn't
wait to bring my fiancé' home to meet the family. Mom
and I had a woman-to-woman talk about marriage. The
entire family was excited. But it was my Mom, I held to
the highest standard, because she had already

experienced
marriage
life for
many years.
It was after
I brought
Garfield
home, I
knew that
Mom
approved.

It wasn't long before we set the wedding date. I didn't ask Mom to help with the wedding expenses because money wasn't available. The wedding was held on October 3, 1970. Dad, Mom and a host of other relatives came to help us celebrate. I can still see Mom, in a blue suite with a white blouse looking so good. And for a special blessing, Mom gave me something blue. Mom told me that there would be some good and not so good times.

She told me, "Don't start anything that I don't want to finish". Mom shared some advice on cooking meals, for Garfield and keeping house, as we prepared later on for our first child. I would call home sometimes when I was upset with Garfield. Instead of siding with me, she would take his side on the matter. She really loves her son-in-law. Mom would come to visit us after our first child was born.

She always loved cooking sweet potato pie. Mom would tell me that the way to a man's heart was through his stomach. That was because she loved to cook and I didn't. Sometimes I would call home to get her recipe for making those good old sweet potato pies and turkey stuffing. I would usually call Mom just before Thanksgiving or Christmas holiday. I did learn a lot from the advice that Mom gave me. She also gave me advice on taking care of my children when they were young.

It's Time to Leave the Nest

Mom is an amazing woman. She has given me so much. Mom tried to prepare me for what was ahead for me in my future life. She taught me to be the best that I could be. I saw how hard Mom worked during her life; I wanted to take a different path. As I prepared for my graduation, I wanted Mom to attend my graduation.

But because she had two of us graduating on the same evening, she chose to attend Clarence's graduation. I was so disappointed that she did not go with me. Dad did go to my graduation. I felt that she should have been with me. I did get past that. In my senior year, a representative from the Federal Bureau of Investigations came to my high school to recruit persons to go to Washington. D.C. to work for the bureau.

I came home that day after school so excited about being accepting to work for the F.B.I. Mom and I talked about it and she gave me her blessing. I filled out the application, which was about fourteen pages back and front. Once everything was complete, I mailed it in. I didn't get an answer right away. After high school, I was sure that I didn't want to attend college, so I decided to take a trade; to become an Operator.

Once I complete the course, I decided that I really didn't want to do this trade; it wasn't for me. It would be weeks, until I would hear back from the F.B.I., I had been last to take the test, and then would be employed to work with the bureau. Mom gave me a heart to heart talk and sent me on my way. I was only seventeen years old when I left home.

As time went on, I would return home to visit, Mom would remind me that I left home at an early age. I truly believed that she did want me to go, but really didn't want her oldest girl to leave home. I thank God for her wisdom and teaching. I thank you Mom for giving me the opportunity to be the best person that I could be. Before Mom became ill, she told me that she was very proud of me.

Summertime

It's summer time. The memories of the summer time make me think about all of the grand kids coming south at one time or another. My first born, Eric started going to SC at the age of one and a half. I remember taking him down on the train to spend time with his grandparents. Don't ask me how Mom took care of all those kids. Mom also had two other grand kids who were a few months older that Eric.

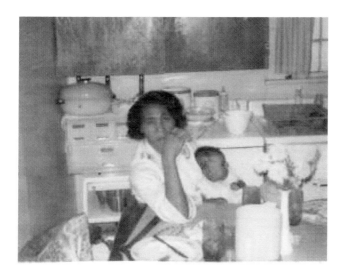

They were Latausha and Latesha, the first set of twin in the famil care of them, because they had been there for a month, and the hospital bill would be so expensive.

So Mom brought the twins home and took care of them. You would have thought that these were Mom's children. Mom really loved all of her grand-children and great-grand's now. One summer, Mom had all of her grand-children there at once. Oh boy, I don't really know how she did it, but she did. Mom has spoiled them all. Once the grand-children became teenagers, they stopped visiting during the summer, but continue to visit during some holidays.

On one occasion, Mom told me that she took her grand-child Ingrid to Lake Junaluska, NC, to a conference. Ingrid asked Mom was that heaven; where they were.

Ingrid thought the cross that was trimmed in light, was where heaven was.   Kisha would also attend the conference as well, along with Latausha and Latesha. One summer, I decide to drive down to the conference with two of my grand-children, Ceirra and Eric Jr. I finally got to see what Ingrid was speaking about. It was a peaceful place. Those were fun memories of my trip to Lake Junaluska, NC.

God Showed Me It Was Dementia

I first started to notice Mom was changing when we were in Florida attending my niece's graduation. Mom was eating and her silverware fell on the floor and she continued to eat with her hands. My brother Clarence, asked me to go get her some more silverware and I did. I then realized that Mom would never be the same again. I

mentioned to the family that something was wrong with Mom.

I also noticed the change at a Thanksgiving holiday gathering. Mom was angry at all of us; especially me. This year the family decided that it was time to give Mom a break from preparing the holiday dinner. Mom wasn't going to have this. Mom continued to give me a look of disapproval. Once she got over being angry, everything was alright.

Mom was diagnosed with Dementia in 2007. I knew something had happened to the Mom that I knew and loved all my life. That year I'll never forget. I didn't want to believe it. At first I didn't want to accept her illness, but as time went on I understood her better. It has been especially hard for me because I'm not there with her. Oh what a shock, but in my mind I'm thinking this is not happening to my loving Mother and wife who has given so much of herself.

I Miss You Mother

I still go home every chance I get. But the Mom I once knew is no longer there. I miss you Mom. It's extremely hard to see you this way. I try so hard to hold back the tears. I won't question God to ask the reason why. Just give me the strength to endure it all until the end. I feel like this wasn't the way it was supposed to be.

Help me Lord, so that I may help someone else that's in the same state that my loving Mother is in. Help me Lord to be able to handle when she no longer knows who I am. Keep my Mother in your loving care. I miss you Mother and I'll always cherish the good times that we shared together.

On a good day, she still knows who her parents are. Mom often says early on that most of her family members were gone. Where did my Mother go? She sounds so normal on the telephone when I call.

Acts of Kindness
MOM GAVE IT ALL

Acts of kindness comes in many ways. Mom showed so much kindness. If you needed something, all you had to do was to ask. She would give you her last dime. Mom shared so much with so many people. During the Christmas season, Mom would give very family member a card and a gift. Mom gave every child and grandchild a gift for their birthdays and sent us cards and gifts for our anniversaries as well. That's just how she was. Mom didn't drive, but she always managed to go visit her sick family members.

Back in the early 70's, Mom came to visit me. I was living with a wonderful lady, Mrs. Sadie Walker. Mom came by the home where I was staying at the time, and met Mrs. Walker; the two of them really hit it off from the start. Mom and Mrs. Walker kept in touch until she passed away. Mom still has the card that Mrs. Walker sent her for Mother's Day one year.

She wasn't a stranger when it came to meeting people. When my Aunt Eunice passed away, Mom felt like

she had to become closer to Eunice's children. She helped
them out as much as she could. One of Aunt Eunice son's,
Billie Joe, had gotten into some trouble and was
incarcerated. He would write Mom and she would write
him back.

Billie Joe told me that Mom would send him a card
for Christmas and put some money in it. He stated that
Mom supported him and gave him words of
encouragement. Billie Joe gives part of the credit for his
new walk with Christ to his Aunt Alma, my Mother, who
never stopped encouraging him to change his way of life. I
will say this for Mom is that she thanks God today for Billie
Joe's faith, love for God and how he allows God to use
him.

Touching Love Lessons of Life

I'm so thankful for all the touching love lessons of life that my Mom taught me. As I think back, Mom didn't punish us much. She would always say, wait until your Dad comes home. Mom was tough in her own way. Mom has always been a strong woman.   I never saw Mom cry. If she cried, she didn't let me see her. I often wondered about that. She had so much courage and faith in God, and that is why she is still here today. Mom lived the life that God wanted her to live, to be the person that she is today, even with Dementia, she still gives God the highest praise.

I would think in my mind, that when I grow up I want to be just like my Mom, tough as leather. Mom was the rock that held the family together. Mom has been not perfect by no means. Mom never drank or smoked. But she did enjoy having fun. Mom was a home body and she didn't do much socializing, unless it was church related. She was just Mom, taking care of the family.

Good Days and Bad Days:
"I DON'T HAVE NO RIGHT TO GRUMBLE"

Mom has good days and bad days but through it all she always said I have no right to grumble. I do try to live by what Mom says. This just blows my mind. Mom is battling through this disease of Dementia but she never complains about how she feels. When I call home, it makes me feel even better to hear her voice. Mom is most always in a cheerful mood.

She doesn't realize how this just makes my day. I really miss her answering the telephone, as she doesn't answer it anymore. It's hard for her to remember things when people call. I do miss that. Through the bad days, I realize that I'm still blessed to have both parents. On a great day, Mom can still tell you who you are and her birthday.

Precious Memories
Oh So Sweet Tears for Mom

As I write this story, the tears are rolling down my face. It's the love that I have for my Mom that I will always treasure the wonderful life and memories of her close to my heart. I only wish I could get her back the way she was. If you still have your Mom, please love her, visit her, or just call her as often as you can.

You don't miss something until you no longer have it. I shall hold these precious memories close to my heart. No one can take these memories away from me. I recall years ago, I would travel with Mom and Dad on trips to Florida and Lake Junaluska North Carolina. Mom loved to travel.

Some of the most fun-filled times were when we would travel to Florida to visit my brother Larry. One year Mom told me I beat them there. She was so surprised. I just wanted to be close to her. I knew that she and Dad would be traveling to Florida. The joke was on them because I beat them there.

We had a wonderful time, it was the Easter holiday. Mom traveled on several occasions with her brother S.T. Parks (Sweet); they were extremely close. They would also travel to Georgia, on the third weekend in August for their annual homecoming at her home church, Mulberry C.M.E Church. The family would come from many states for a good old time for dinner and fellowship. I couldn't wait to speak with Mom to see how the trip went. As usual, Mom had a great time going to Georgia.

Mom and Dad used to attend the church conference and retreat at Lake Junaluska, North Carolina. They always had a great time. Mom would take the grandkids with them. The conference and retreat was always held in the summer months. One year, I decided to make the trip down to attend the retreat. It was amazing. Mom also made many trips to visit us in Washington, DC and Maryland. We loved when Mom came to town, because we knew that she would be cooking some of her favorite dishes.

Mom's So Happy
AUGUST 4, 2014

Mom's so happy. When I call she has so much joy in her voice. I shared with her that I had spent the weekend attending Garfield's 50th Class reunion. I told her that we danced the night away. Mom laughed and said, "Enjoy your life". That meant so much to me. Those are the days when she brings me joy. It's hard to believe that she has Dementia when I call home. Earlier in the day I had spoken with my sister Lydia; it was her birthday.

Lydia was upset because Mom wasn't doing well that day at the day care. Mom is changing each day. I spoke with Lydia and told her that God is going to take care of Mom and that He would work it out. I tried to comfort Lydia on the telephone. I know it's extremely hard to see Mom in that state. I really try to be strong, but the strongest person gets weak sometimes.

I can't recall what was playing on the radio but while I was listening to the song the tears just started rolling down my face, uncontrollable, and I could not stop. I pray every day that God will help me stay focused on the wonderful memories that we have shared together. It won't be easy to let Mom go.

My First Trip to Augusta Georgia

THE ELAM- PARKS FAMILY REUNION

It was August 2012 when I decided to attend my Mom's Annual Elam Parks Reunion. This year was especially important because Mom wasn't able to attend due to her illness. She's unable to travel now. I thought what a treat this is going to be. I'll finally get to go to my Mom's hometown. The reunion was held in August in Augusta Georgia. Oh boy was I in for treat.

I drove down to Greer, where I met up with Mom's sister Bobbie and her husband Willie. We arrived at the reunion based hotel. I would finally get to meet some of the relatives that Mom had spoken about after all these years. Mom's family members were from several states all over the place. The highlight of the trip was the tour of Mom's hometown Lincolnton, Georgia.

Oh how I wish Mom was able to attend this reunion. We gathered to attend the cook-out. The food was so good. I met some of my ancestor's family members, whom parents were slaves. We toured the cemetery, were a lot of my ancestors were buried. The close of the reunion was at the church, Mulberry C.M.E. Church, where my grand-daddy Willie Parks belonged there and now he is buried there. I also saw where Mom taught in a one room building.

I got to see my grand-daddy's grave for the first time. Thinking back when grand-daddy died I was still in high school. Mom decided not to take any of us to the home-going service. I always wondered why we couldn't attend. Mom often spoke with her cousin Lillie Bell, who was from Lincolnton, Georgia as well. Lillie Bell and Mom were very close. Cousin Lillie Bell and her family would drive up to visit us often. I did get to see Cousin Lillie Bell's daughter, Lillian and some of the other family members. This trip made up for everything that I had missed. Those memories I'll hold dear and near my heart.

Mom's Final Wishes for Her Homegoing Service

This part of my story is somewhat difficult to write, but I'm going to share it anyway. Many years ago during one of my visits home, Mom decided to discuss her wishes to be carried out after she passes. Mom wanted Alma Jane and I to do her obituary together. Lydia is to take care of the deals at the mortuary. Larry and Clarence are to take care of the details for her final resting place.

I indicated to Mom why me? Mom told me that's what she wanted me to do. Mom would often say laughingly that she wanted a private funeral. Only those persons that we invited were to attend. Mom often said that she wanted everybody to give her flowers while she's still alive. I always tried to do that.

Mom also indicated that she wanted to be taken back to Georgia. Many years, before I left home Mom, gave me a bible marker with her favorite scripture on it. It is the 23rd Psalm and her favorite song is, "I will trust in the

Lord until I die". I do plan to carry out her wishes as she asked.

The Song on the Radio
THAT MAKES ME SAD

One Sunday, on my way home from church, a song came on the radio and tears began to roll down my face. I really didn't understand what was happening to me at that time. The song was telling me that God was preparing me for something I wouldn't handle. I guess that's what God was trying to tell me through a song about my Mom. It wasn't long after, I learned that Mom was diagnosed with Dementia and I knew that's what God was trying to tell me through that song on the radio.

As Mom's Dementia begun to get worse, she would sit by the telephone all day long. Mom started misplacing items. She would talk about her family history over and over. I first knew that something was wrong when Mom would get so angry with me.

Dementia

Dementia, you came to steal, kill and destroy. You are inside my Mom's brain. Who knew when you would come into her life? You came without being invited into her life. I wish I could have sent you away. You have taken her past, present and her future memories from her. I don't think I'll ever like you. Why oh, why did you have to attack her brain?

Mom is such a kind loving, wife, mother, grand-mother and great-grand mother. I wish that it was a cure for you, Dementia. I won't let you attack me and anyone else that I love. If it was up to me, I would put you away where you won't hurt anyone else. You have taken my Mother away from me; never to return in this life. But she still keeps hanging on.

Dementia, day by day, I see you take everything away from my Mother. One day someone will find a cure for you, and we will bury you where you are supposed to be. Dementia you have to go back to where you came from. Hopefully one day you will be found DOA.

As I began to write this book, I prayed that God would give me the wisdom and the knowledge to compose several poems. This poem says it all, about how I feel about the disease.

It's So Hard to Say Goodbye
AUGUST 18, 2014

As the weeks go by, I have a strong feeling that the end is closer than I want to realize. I think about Mom every day. I try not to worry, but that's impossible. I see her in my dreams. I want to wake up quickly and erase that dream. I'm planning to go on a trip, but my heart feels like something is going to happen while I'm gone. I pray that God will continue to give me the strength that I need and that everyone including Mom will be alright. I never thought my parents would live to be in their eighties and nineties. It truly is a blessing. The longer you have your parents around, the harder it is to let them go. Each night I pray for Mom especially, but Dad as well. God has a plan for my Mom and Dad. The memories are so sweet.

This short story doesn't cover Mom's entire life, but just this special part that I wanted to share. So for now, I will wait on the unthinkable, the end of her life with this disease. I pray that the end will be pleasant and painless. My life won't ever be the same, so for now I'll say so long, but no good bye. We shall meet again.

Mom's Trip to Myrtle Beach SC
Celebration 65th Wedding Anniversary

Oh boy we did so enjoy the grand celebration of our parents 65th Wedding anniversary party. I decided to plan and organize their anniversary in Myrtle Beach. All of my siblings were there to celebrate their anniversary. I planned a fish fry on Friday night and a banquet on Saturday. We had family, friends and special guests to attend. Mom's sister Bobbie was there with her husband Willie.

Mom's nieces Brenda Faye and Debbie were there for the celebration as well. Brenda and Debbie played a special part in preparing the food on Friday night. My

daughter Kisha and her children Brianna and Andre attended along with a close friend. Mom had already been diagnosed with Dementia. She enjoyed herself although she was out of her surroundings and wanted to go home. That was the last trip away from home. Mom made it through the celebration that weekend.

Dad and Mom were showered with gifts and cards. Mom was all smiles. She stuck close to Dad like glue and she was in her own world. She was setting there with there with the man she had married for sixty- five years- plus. We all had a grand time.

Joy through the Pain

As I look back, I realize that Mom has brought me and so many others much joy in their lives. My joy is celebrating the wonderful times and events in my life that we shared together. Mom supported me in my business when I started sell Mary Kay Products. When I left home to start a new life and career, Mom encouraged me to be the best that I could be. She wanted me to remember the lessons of life and what she had taught me.

Mom told me to hold my head high, find a church to join, and to watch the persons that I associated with. She encouraged me to be a lady at all times, and she reminded me not to allow a man to disrespect me, but always treat me like a lady. Mom told me to find a gentleman who would treat me,  with the upmost of respect, and I did.

Priceless Treasures:

Recipes, Poems, and Pictures

Priceless Treasures:

Mom's Recipes

Homemade Crock Pot Macaroni

1-Box of 8oz Macaroni
2Tsp Wesson Oil
3 cups sharp cheese
1 can milk (large)
1 -1/2 cup of sweet milk
½ cup of butter salt & pepper

Steps:
Grease crock pot
Mix first then pour all ingredients in the
crock pot
Cook for 3-4 hours on low

© Alma Parks Mills

Homemade Pound Cake

1 cup butter or margarine
3 cups sugar
2 tablespoons lemon juice
(Juice and rid of one lemon)
½ cup cooking oil
5 large eggs
½ teaspoon salt
1 cup sweet milk
3 -2/3 cups of cake flour

Steps:
Mix cream butter and sugar

Add oil/ 2-tablespoon of lemon

Bake for 1 ½ hour on 350 degrees

© Alma Parks Mills

Mom's Sweet Potato Pie

4 round sweet potatoes
2 eggs
2 teaspoon butter
1 cup of milk
1 cup of sweet
1 teaspoon- cinnamon
1 pinch of nutmeg (to taste)
2 cups of mixture for per pie

Steps:

Bake @ 350 degrees for 45 Minutes or until done

© Alma Parks Mills

Banana Pudding

6 Bananas
1 box-Vanilla wafers
8oz Sour cream (nonfat)
9oz Non-dairy cool whip topping lite
2 package small instant vanilla pudding
(Sugar free)
3 cups of milk 1percent or skim

Steps:

Mix at a slow speed/ mix pudding mix with milk until thick

Add sour cream & cool whip and blend

Layer 13x9" casserole dish/ with wafers and bananas

½ of pudding mixture

Repeat and end with pudding mixtures/ top with cool whip
on top

© Alma Parks Mills

Priceless Treasures:

Poems

I Had to Pray

As time passed I would become very depressed when I came home to visit Mom. I had to pray and ask God to help me through this.

It was during this difficult time that I decided to write this book. God helped to me write several poems that sum up how I really feel about her illness. I'm sharing these poems and praying that they may help someone deal with this disease of Dementia.

Love is a Gift from God

Love is a gift from God. It is far more precious that any material thing one could ever hope to possess. It can't be purchased, for along with all of the best things in life it is free.

Its magic can change a dreary world into a heaven on earth. Its radiance is beyond human power of description. It is not restricted by race, creed or public opinion and has nothing to do with physical appearance, for beauty is in the eye of the beholder. There is no fault or shortcoming that love cannot overcome with charity and understanding it does not imprison, but rather in loving, one is set free.

There is no limit to what love can accomplish, for its depth fine qualities that would otherwise remain disputed.

Author unknown

I found this writing in some of Mom's things when I was home in March 2014. I don't know who wrote it, but the words really explain that Love is truly a gift from God.

Mom I Don't Want You Go Away

Mom don't go away, I'll miss you so

If you only knew how I will miss our talks

Mom I know you were not put her to stay forever,

But Mom I still don't want you to go away.

I'm too far to get there quickly.

So you can't go away until I get there.

Each time I see you I just want to hug you and not let you

go.

It's so hard to see you looking so sad and confused.

So don't go away until I give you the biggest kiss.

I'll miss you so much.

My life won't ever be the same, so don't go away anytime

soon.

I know it's only God's plan, but Mom don't go away.

It just breaks my heart in a thousand of pieces to see you

this way.

Written by Gloria L. Mills Battle-September 9, 2014

You Bring Me Joy

You bring me Joy, when I'm down

Oh, so much Joy, when I lose my way,

I think of your smiling face.

Don't go too far away

If I can't see your face

I'll always remember you everyday

My joy, my joy

I just love you Mom

You bring me Joy,

My Joy, you are my joy

Written by Gloria L. Mills Battle September 9, 2014

Joy and Pain

Joy and pain, it won't ever be the same

It was just like it was yesterday when the Dementia stole
your Joy for pain

I know that your love will last forever,

And will always remain the same some joy and pain

Suddenly the things I see is hurting you so badly

How come the things that make us happy sometimes
make us sad?

Well it seems like joy has turned to pain

Joy and pain is like sunshine and rain

Nothing ever remains the same

That's when we go through life with up and downs

But through the Joy, God brings us the pain

Mom

My Mom has made me laugh

Made me cry

Wiped my tears

Hugged me tight

Watch me succeed

See me fail

Cheered me on

Kept me going strong

And drove me crazy

Mom you are a promise from God

You will have a fiend forever

-Author unknown-

A Daughter's Prayer for Her Mom

Dear Lord,

Help my Mom to get through the pain until the end of her journey. Give her a peace and joy through this pain. Lord, as my Mom transitions through, let her not suffer. In her mind, Lord, she is lost here on earth. Lord, I pray that she will have no more worries in this world. Lord, I don't really understand why she was given this, but I do know for sure that you have her in your loving arms.

Lord, please do not let her suffer not one second, not one minutes, or not one hour. Cover her Lord from any hurt, pain or danger. And Lord when that final hour has come, give her a better home up above. Where there will be no more Dementia. Lord, I pray that you will hear my prayer, in the precious name of Jesus.

Priceless Treasures:

Pictures